CYCLING TO WORK

Cycling to Work

A beginner's guide

Rory McMullan

Green Books

Published in 2007
by Green Books, Foxhole, Dartington
Totnes, Devon TQ9 6EB

Reprinted 2007

Design concept by Julie Martin jmartin1@btinternet.com

Photos were kindly supplied by (and are the copyright of):
Raleigh, Paul McMullan / Channel News Service,
Nick Turner / Sustrans, J Bewley / Sustrans, Pfizer, Moore Large,
Marin, Powacycle, Madison, Sturmey, and www.urban75.com.

Printed by Cambrian Printers, Aberystwyth, UK.

Text printed on 100% post-consumer waste paper. Covers are
made from 75% recycled material.

DISCLAIMER: The advice in this book is believed to be correct
at the time of printing, but the authors and publishers accept
no liability for actions inspired by this book.

ISBN 978 1 900322 12 6

To discuss a possible bulk purchase of this book,
please phone Green Books on 01803 863260

Contents

Acknowledgements

There are a multitude of good reasons to get back on your bike, and fortunately there are plenty of organisations and individuals who work tirelessly to encourage more people to do what is good for them, good for society and good for the planet.

This book is dedicated to these people, for without their efforts, facilities for cyclists would be nowhere near as good.

Many of these cycle advocates provided their help, advice and support in publishing this handbook.

Particular thanks to Carlton Reid, Bikeforall.net; Nick Harvey, BikeWeek; Paul McMullan, Channel News and Pictures; Dave Holladay, CTC; David Dansky, Cycle Training UK; James Steward, Cyclepods; Dolly Sura and Denis Canning, GlaxoSmithKline; Claire Fleming, Nottinghamshire County Council; John Gough and James Graham, Pfizer UK; Michael Hartley, T-Mobile; Mike Sloecome, Urban75.com; Shane Collins, Urban Green Fair; and special thanks to the contributors of case studies. Thanks are also due to the following organisations: Association for Commuter Transport, ATB Sales, Bikemagic.com, CTC, Cycling England, Discount Bicycles, Leeds City Council, London Cycling Campaign, Powacycle, Raleigh Bicycles, SheCycles.com, Stratton Cycles and Wiltshire County Council.

And finally, a huge thank-you to Jon Clift, Amanda Cuthbert and John Elford and all of the Green Books team, who did virtually all the work on this book.

Chapter 1

WHY CYCLE?

If you are thinking "I can't cycle, I live too far from work, I don't want to breathe polluted air, I'm too old, I don't want to get hot and sweaty, I'm unfit . . ." this book might just change your mind.

You're better off by bike!

Cycling keeps you healthy and makes you feel better

Regular exercise helps people feel better; studies show that cyclists have fewer days absence and are more productive at work. On average, regular cyclists:

- add over 2 years to their life expectancy
- have the general fitness and health of someone 10 years younger
- are 50% less likely to experience depression

Doctors advise a minimum of 30 minutes moderate exercise a day to keep fit; if you feel unfit, start slowly and work your way up to longer journeys – you will soon gain confidence and fitness. Don't drive to the gym – cycle to work!

Cycling means a less polluted journey

Research shows that car occupants are exposed to 2-3 times the level of pollution of cyclists.

Cyclists ride up above the most polluted air. Motor traffic produces a cocktail of noxious gases that are linked to cancer and respiratory diseases, and you are actually most at risk from air pollution when driving in heavy traffic, as the ventilation system sucks in the emissions from the exhaust of the vehicle in front.

Cycling helps you lose weight

Whilst our calorie intake has hardly risen in the past 30 years, almost 60% of us are either overweight or obese; this is almost entirely due to reduced levels of exercise, which have fallen dramatically with the rise in car use and parallel fall in cycling.

Losing weight is often seen as the best way to improve self-confidence, whereas fad diets often only work in the short term; cycling not only burns the calories – it is also good for your health and general sense of well-being.

Cycling at a moderate pace of about 10mph burns on average 400 calories per hour for women and 450 per hour for men – about the same as an aerobics session.

Cycling saves you money

The AA estimates that the average car costs 41p per mile to run; and cyclists don't need to pay parking or congestion charges, which operate in or are planned for most major UK cities.

Compare the costs of running a car or the value of your season ticket with the £250 it costs to buy a good-quality bike and equipment, which will last you three or more years; you can easily see how much money cycling to work will save you, even if you only use your bike for part of the journey.

You don't have to sell the car to start cycling (most regular cyclists are also motorists), but a bike can often replace one car of a two-car family. If you live in a major city with good public transport you might not need a car at all, as a bicycle can be faster and more convenient.

Cycling is quicker and offers more flexibility

Cyclists are the most punctual of all employees: traffic jams do not affect them, neither do train delays. Even if you don't get snarled up in a traffic jam, parking a car can be a nightmare, whereas a bicycle can usually be parked right outside your workplace.

Speed and reliability are the reasons why urgent deliveries are made by cycle courier in the world's busiest cities.

The roads of major cities and towns are almost at gridlock during peak times; average speeds have hardly risen since 1900, and in some cases have fallen. Because a bicycle is incredibly space-efficient, if we can convert unnecessary car trips to cycling, then our congestion levels will fall.

Cycling is cool

Over the past fifty years cycling has had a bad press: it was the forgotten mode of transport, the car was king, everybody who didn't have a car was perceived to be poor, and people felt defined by the car they drove. But things are changing; these days mobile phones, Blackberrys and iPods are the most important accessories for the image-conscious, and cycling is becoming part of this new fashion. Cycling, and the healthy, environmentally-friendly lifestyle it represents, is now used to advertise mobile phones, laptops, cameras and, ironically, cars.

In London over 450,000 trips are made by bike each day.

Boasting about how quickly you get to work takes on a whole new dimension when you ride a bike. Cyclists spend less on transport but on average earn more than the average income; a typical cyclist is

a rich, healthy, image-conscious professional; no wonder that high-profile politicians and presidents of global corporations want to be seen to cycle to work.

Cycling is enjoyable

Cycling can beat driving for pure enjoyment; in the past few years local authorities have invested heavily in cycle lanes, many of which go through lovely areas like parks, or along rivers.

THE WIDER PICTURE

Cycling helps to combat climate change

Transport accounts for over 20% of CO_2 emissions, more than half of which comes from private cars.

Many scientific studies have shown global warming and climate change to be real, and it is now fully accepted by governments worldwide that we have a pressing problem. The Stern Report, commissioned by the Treasury, estimates that we have to cut our emissions by 60% in the next thirty years to save us from the worst consequences of climate change. Cycling to work is not going to solve climate change on its own, but it is part of the solution.

Global warming and the end of the oil age are challenges of immense proportions, but we can help to solve these huge problems by making many small changes in the way we live. We have to start making these changes now; cycling more and driving less is one of the easiest and most enjoyable.

Our cities

There is no doubt that cars provide fast, comfortable and flexible personal transport and have a valuable place in our transport system, but their sheer popularity causes serious environmental problems. Changing from a car to a bike, even for just some of your journeys, will help improve the environment in which we live and work.

Our public spaces

If we could convert many unnecessary car trips to bicycle trips there would be a lot fewer cars on the streets, making more room for quality public space in our towns. Bicycles are not only the most energy-efficient transportation machine that man has invented, they are also among the most space-efficient.

In metropolitan areas space is at a premium, and a car-based transport system needs a lot of space. The average car uses approximately four times the space of the average home: this includes parking spaces at the home, workplace, shopping centre, supermarket, and town centre; and these parking spaces are on average only occupied about 20% of the time!

Cars need a lot of road space. Road capacity is designed for rush hour, so although city streets may not be busy at midnight, during peak times congestion is a major problem, which is not only inefficient in time but also in fuel.

Bicycles take up less than 20% of the space of a moving car, and a comparatively tiny amount of parking space – a folding bike uses even less. If we convert just a few trips from car to bike, especially during rush hour, some of the space that was used for cars can be turned into quality public space for community recreation.

Air and noise pollution

Reducing the amount of cars in our cities will improve the air quality. Traffic noise causes stress, and in big cities there is almost no escape; but with fewer car trips and more bicycle trips we can have quieter, cleaner urban environments.

Safer communities

If each one of us gets on our bike we will reduce the number of cars on the roads, making a safer environment for the community and reducing the risk of accidents.

On average 3,500 people die in car accidents in the UK every year.

Chapter 2

CAN YOU CYCLE TO WORK?

To be honest, the sun is not always shining, big hills are difficult to climb, and not all offices have showers; but with the right route and the right kit, these things are no big deal.

Planning the best route

Even if you live a long way from work it may still be possible to use your bike for all or part of the journey: you can take your bike on buses and trains, buy a folding bike, or leave your bike in a locker.

You will quickly discover that the routes you use by car are not usually the ones you would choose to use by bike. There are often great shortcuts that you can take on a bike, and sometimes the longer way can actually be better, e.g. if there is a route beside a river, or through a park; your journey to work might take more time, but will become the highlight of the day.

First you'll need a good map. Check to see if your local authority, local cycle groups or bicycle shop have cycle-specific maps with cycle-friendly routes marked on them – they almost certainly do. Look on the internet for maps and route advice for your area, and Google maps can be used to look at your route (see also Chapter 7, page 75).

Start by getting a high-quality cycle route map – try asking your local council, or download from www.cyclemaps.org.uk or www.lifecycleuk.org.uk.

If you work for an organisation that has a Travel Plan Officer, then you can ask for advice on the surrounding cycle routes. Most Human Resources or Facilities departments should also be able to help. There may also be a Bicycle User Group at work; they often meet once a month after work, and can help you find cycle buddies to show you the best routes. Try to chat to anyone who cycles to work – tell them you are thinking about cycling, and you'll find that they will be keen to share their secrets, just as you will be when you find that super shortcut through the park. If you can't find anyone to chat to, then it can be just as satisfying to be the pioneer.

Look at your current route, and if you are driving along a high-speed six-lane bypass or really busy road, look to see if there are parks, smaller residential roads or paths that you could use instead.

HELMET-HAIR DAYS

"My shortest route to work is about 6 miles, but I prefer a slightly longer option with less traffic. There is a shower at work, but I rarely need to use it as I don't really sweat and in the mornings when I'm feeling a bit dopey anyway I ride slowly. I have shoes in the office, and take clothes, lunch and handbag in panniers.

You quickly discover which clothes can make the journey without getting too creased. I have mentally divided my work wardrobe into two parts: 'clothes to wear on days when I cycle' and 'clothes to wear when I have to drive'. There's loads of smart-looking travel clothing that is ideal for the purpose – I have loads of Rohan stuff. My colleagues have got used to me hanging my clothes around the office to dry, and my helmet-hair days!" – Anu Lappalainen, Mapping Services Manager, Hampshire.

It is not a good idea to try a new route for the first time when you are rushing to get to work on time, so give it a try one weekend and look on it as good exercise. Once you have found a route you like, try to do it once without getting lost, and time yourself. Add about 10 minutes to allow for getting your bike out and locking it at your destination.

Integrating bikes with trains, buses and cars

If you live too far from work to cycle all the way, you can take a folding bicycle on a train and cycle to and from the station. There may be other options: for example, a bicycle combined with a bus or train, or a friend's or colleague's car. If you are lucky, your home and your workplace will be close to stations on the same

line – then you'll probably find a bicycle and train combination is the quickest way to commute.

Bicycles can be taken free of charge onto most trains; they usually fit in the space for wheelchairs (if not occupied), or in the guard's van on high-speed trains. However not all trains have space for bikes, especially at rush hour, when many trains in London do not accept them. All is not lost, however, as a folding bicycle is always allowed, and if it is compact enough you can even take it on a bus or tube.

Folding bikes can also be fitted into the boot of most cars. 'Park and ride' takes on a whole new meaning with a bike in the boot: parking on the edge of town and cycling is usually the fastest and certainly cheapest way into the centre, avoiding both traffic jams and excessive parking charges.

A good folding bike can be expensive, and is sometimes not as comfortable to ride as a full-sized bike; an alternative is to have

UNSCENTED BABY WIPES

"I ride to work – though I have yet to manage more than twice a week – but it is 15 miles each way, which takes me about two hours a day. I do it because I enjoy it, and as I work for an environmental charity feel I should set an example. I'd do it more if my other half didn't ride to work as well and we didn't need to manage the children. I keep a supply of clothes, coat, shoes, shower / wash stuff and food at work. I am lucky enough to be able to have a shower when I get there, (after 15 miles in the morning I generally need one!), but I understand unscented baby wipes are great. My bike shed is not great – it is a small, quietish site but in a well-used area, and there are always people about. It takes a bit of planning, but in my opinion it's well worth the effort." – Karen Lifford, The Woodland Trust, Lincolnshire

two bikes. By riding one bike from your home to the station and keeping a second bike at the station close to your work, you can have all the convenience of a folding bicycle without the hassle of carrying it on the train.

A two-bike combination is ideal where a bus trip makes up the bulk of the distance, as British buses have yet to adopt the bicycle rack on the front that is common elsewhere.

Looking good when you get there

Many people don't cycle because they worry about looking like a sweaty beast or drenched rat if it rains on the way to work. Many workplaces now have showers; if yours doesn't, you could point out the advantages to your employer:

- the cost savings on parking spaces (which cost up to £2,000 per year to maintain)
- the extra productivity of a healthy workforce
- the increased punctuality of cyclists compared to other commuters

They just might install one for you!

There are, however, some occasions when it is not easy, like going for an interview, or a meeting off-site where getting changed on arrival would be inappropriate. If you are not up for changing in the toilets in a café, the solution is to either cycle more slowly so you don't sweat, or to take the bus or car instead.

Many workplaces also have lockers where you can leave a clean set of clothes; it is quite easy to carry a towel, toiletries and a change of clothes with you on a bike in panniers or a backpack. Breathable waterproof clothing will keep you dry when it is raining (see Chapter 4, pages 41-48).

If you leave your work shoes at the office it saves a lot of weight in your bag; then all you need to carry is a change of clothes to start work looking smart and feeling fresh. Try to get to work 10 or 15 minutes early to give yourself a chance to cool down, brush up and change clothes.

Don't forget however that cycling to work a few times a week will help you lose a few excess pounds and although you don't have to look like Kate Moss to look good, you will feel better and the change will probably be noticed by your loved ones. So maybe a few pounds off the beer belly might be worth a few hairs out of place once in a while.

Working up to the commute

How far is too far to cycle? It depends on how fit you are, how many hills there are, and how long you are prepared to take to get there. For a fit beginner forty minutes is about the limit: in forty minutes on relatively flat terrain a beginner cyclist should be able to cover up to eight miles at a sedate pace.

Not all of us are 19 years old, super-fit with trim bodies to match, but if your office is less than five miles from your home, then no matter how old or unfit you may feel, why not give it a try.

Work up to it: practise at weekends, either on the route to work or just playing about with the family. Remember that cycling is not just for commuting. It is a sport and a leisure activity too, so a bit of practice will be fun – but the enjoyment is not always obvious if you are out of breath and sweating like a pig – just try to remember that its good for you!

Finally, when you feel good about it, the weather looks good, and the evenings are long, go for it: try to cycle all the way to work. See if you can convince one of your colleagues or neighbours whose workplace is near yours to join you in your quest, as a bit of company will make it much more enjoyable.

A great way to get to know other cyclists at your workplace is to organise a group ride during Bike Week, the second week of June. Explore the local area for pleasant routes, and go on a group ride during the lunch break or after work. It's great fun, and a perfect way to find potential cycle buddies. Posters and other promotional materials are available free from the Bike Week website.

Check with your company if they are organising a bikers' breakfast or rides for Bike Week – a fry-up can be a welcome incentive.

See www.bikeweek.org.uk for more details.

Chapter Three

BUYING A BIKE

In the past twenty years bicycle design has undergone a revolution that has seen the introduction of bikes that can tackle all types of terrain, with space age materials, multiple gears, suspension and disc brakes. Walk into a bike shop these days and you are likely to see a vast array of bicycles with prices ranging from under £200 to well over £2,000.

But even spending thousands of pounds won't guarantee you get the best bike for your needs; for instance, an expensive downhill bike with big wide knobbly tyres, disc brakes and long travel suspension might be perfect for riding over rough terrain down a mountainside, but will be slow and heavy in the city.

Where to buy a bike

You don't need to go to a bicycle shop to buy a bicycle, as you can get them almost anywhere: online, at supermarkets, in department stores and by mail order. The advantage of buying your bike from a dedicated bicycle shop is that the sales staff are likely to be more knowledgeable and helpful in choosing the right bike for your needs.

The advantage of buying online, from Price-Drop TV, large retail parks or supermarkets, is that you can sometimes save money. The risk you take is that if you are unable to try the bike first you will not be able to check if it is the right size. If you don't know much about bicycle design and components, the bike you buy might be cheap but not actually very good value. You generally get what you pay for, and if a bike looks too cheap to be true it probably is, as it is likely to be made with the cheapest parts and might be heavy and unreliable.

If you decide to buy through mail order or online, the bike is likely to be delivered only part-assembled and with untuned gears, brakes and wheels. Although most quality online or mail-order companies will tune the bike before they box it, and all that is usually required is straightening the handlebars and putting on the front wheel and pedals (which is quite simple to do), it can seem difficult for the less mechanically proficient. A poorly assembled bike is dangerous to ride.

Finally, brake and gear cables will stretch after about 2-3 weeks of riding. A bike shop will usually give an after-sales service free of charge, and adjust the cables for you. If you buy online or at a supermarket you will need to do this yourself.

How much do bikes cost?

Bikes range hugely in price, but generally speaking a good new commuting bike will cost between £170-£500. The price depends on the type of bike, the components that have been used to build it, the weight and brand. A more expensive bike will shift more smoothly through more gears, will be lighter, and possibly have a more comfortable saddle.

The bike you choose depends amongst other things on your budget, but for around £200 you can buy a pretty good bike to get around town, and an extra £50 will buy you all the extra parts and accessories you need to get started.

Maintaining and servicing the bike will probably cost around £30 a year, depending on how much you use it.

Over all, after calculating depreciation, maintenance and the purchase of accessories, regular urban cycling can cost as little as £150 per year. The savings you make on city centre parking or public transport tickets should cover this cost in a couple of months.

MY £20 BIKE

"I live in West Bridgford in Nottinghamshire, and travel to Derby each day, where I teach. I take the train from Nottingham station, which is more than three-quarters of an hour from my house on foot, and in morning traffic the bus takes about the same time. I bought an old second-hand BSA bicycle for £20 from a local bicycle shop, and now cycle to the station (where I chain the bike up) in less than 15 minutes. My heavy duty D-lock actually cost more than the bike, but it has worked." – Lisa Clark, 27, art teacher, Nottinghamshire.

Cycle to Work: 'Salary sacrifice' schemes

This scheme offers employees the chance to get bicycles and bicycle equipment through their employer at much lower cost than buying direct. **Cycle to Work** is a government tax incentive aimed at encouraging employees to cycle to work. The scheme allows employees to benefit from a long-term loan of a bike and safety equipment completely tax-free. The tax savings can allow employees to save about 50% on the price of a new bike.

This scheme is very easy to set up, and there are many organisations that can help your company, if needed. Ask your Human Resources manager to look into it. For more information see www.bikeforall.net/content/cycle_to_work_scheme.php.

Second-hand bikes

If you are on a low income and £200 would break the bank, then you can save money buying second-hand. Perfectly good bikes can be had for just a few quid: try your local recycling centre. Second-hand bikes are usually found in the local newspaper, on websites like Ebay, from a market or car boot sale, or sometimes reconditioned from your local bike store.

Your safest bet is to buy one that has been reconditioned from your local bike shop, as it will be tuned and ready to go. Stolen bikes often end up for sale in car boot sales or markets, so be careful when buying a second-hand bike – if the bike you purchase was stolen, you will lose it with no compensation.

When buying second-hand, check that the main components like gears and chain-drive work well and smoothly, as these will cost the most to replace. Also check that the handlebars and pedals turn smoothly; if there is a grating sound, it is possible that the ball bearings have gone – replacing any of these is a difficult and expensive job.

Bikes that have been repossessed by the police are often sold at auction. In London this is run by www.greasbys.co.uk.

Size matters

There is a certain amount of personal preference in bike size, so there can be no better advice than to try the bike first before buying it. Nothing beats expert advice – talk to your local bike shop staff, and ask them to set the bike up for you.

As with shoes, getting the right size of bike will make a big difference to your comfort; but unlike shoes, there is a considerable amount of adjustment in the handlebar and saddle height of a bike, so it can be set up for you perfectly.

Bigger is not necessarily better An easy rule to follow when choosing your bike is that you should be able to reach the ground with your toes while sitting in the saddle. For bikes with a cross-bar, when you are standing flat-footed there should be adequate clearance between the cross-bar and your crotch; this is particularly important for guys in case you fall forward onto the bar while riding.

If you like to sit upright, go for the biggest frame that still allows cross-bar clearance. If you prefer more athletic riding, particularly if you like to jump up and down from kerbs and take the odd off-road route, you are safest with maximum clearance; so plump for the smallest possible frame – as long as you can still stretch your legs and the bike isn't so short that it cramps your riding style.

Below is a rough sizing chart of bike size in relation to inside leg – the distance from your crotch to the floor. The frame size is the length of the seat tube (the tube that the seat-post and saddle are fixed into).

	INSIDE LEG		FRAME SIZE SUGGESTED	
	cms	ins	cms	ins
Mountain or hybrid bicycle	61-74	24-29	38	15
	64-76	25-30	41	16
	66-79	26-31	43	17
	69-81	27-32	46	18
	71-84	28-33	48	19
	74-86	29-34	51	20
	81-94	32-37	56	22
	INSIDE LEG		FRAME SIZE SUGGESTED	
	cms	ins	cms	ins
Traditional, Ladies, City bicycle	64-76	25-30	43	17
	69-79	27-31	48	19
	74-84	29-33	53	21
	79-89	31-35	58	23
	INSIDE LEG		FRAME SIZE SUGGESTED	
	cms	ins	cms	ins
Racing, Touring bicycle	71-81	28-32	50	19.5
	76-86	30-34	55	21.5
	81-91	32-36	58	23
	86-97	34-38	62	24.5

What type of bike do you need?

There are many different types of bicycle to choose from, each designed to perform a different function. Before buying a bike you need to consider what you will be using it for. If you want super-fast commuting with the minimum of luggage, a road race bike might be best; or if you are after a more comfortable bike, then a traditional city bike may fit the bill better.

Below is a list of the most suitable bikes for commuting, with general descriptions and the advantages and disadvantages of each. A lower, more aerodynamic posture will be faster as it cuts through the headwind, but may feel uncomfortable to riders who are not used to it; while upright postures are the reverse – very comfortable, but slower as it is harder to push against the wind.

Mountain bikes – all Terrain bikes (ATBs): £60-£3,000

Mountain bikes took the world by storm in the 1990s, and are still the best-selling design of bicycle. When the likes of Gary Fisher and Joe Breeze first started to launch themselves down the rocky slopes of the mountains of Marin County near San Francisco, few would have believed they were starting an industry. The converted old cruiser bikes they used in the 1970s have now morphed into a myriad of incarnations of mountain bike, each designed to cope with a slightly different terrain or riding discipline.

These days, although mountain bikes come in many shapes and sizes, the most suitable types for city riding are cross-country or all-terrain bikes (ATB). These both have tough frames, good brakes, lots of gears, knobbly tyres, suspension forks and sometimes rear suspension. The cross-country bike design is to allow the rider to climb and descend off-road tracks at the fastest speed. The ATB is not as high performance as the cross-country bike, and is designed to withstand the rigours of rough treatment.

Both these designs are easy to control and will work well in the city, although it is recommended to swap the knobbly tyres for 'slicks', which are smooth-tread tyres that offer lower rolling resistance on road.

Advantages Mountain bikes are strong, easy to control, and can be taken off-road at the weekends for a bit of fun.

Disadvantages A good mountain bike has been designed for performance off-road, but it doesn't come with accessories to make city riding more comfortable, like mudguards or a wide saddle. It has a low posture which may be uncomfortable, and off-road parts, like suspension, are expensive and unnecessary for urban cycling. Watch out for the cheap mountain bikes on the market – these can be very heavy, with poor quality components, and would possibly break if actually taken off-road.

Road racing bikes: £200-£6,000

Road racing bikes are designed for speed. They are light, have larger diameter wheels with thin smooth tyres for the minimum of rolling resistance, good brakes, many gears, and usually drop handlebars to make for a very low aerodynamic posture.

Some road bikes now have flat handlebars to give you a slightly more upright posture for added comfort and control – which can be useful in the city.

They usually have a higher gear range than a mountain bike, which makes them faster on the flat, but slightly harder to ride up very steep hills.

Some cycle dispatch couriers in London choose to ride fixed-gear racing bikes. These have no gears, but when the wheel turns, so do the pedals, making for extremely efficient transmission and therefore high speeds on the flat, although steep hills can be a hard slog. These bikes are also more difficult to control.

Advantages Speed. There is no quicker way to ride around a city than on a road racing bike. *Disadvantages* The price can be very high for a good road racing bike, which can make them attractive to thieves. The thin wheels are not strong, making them prone to punctures and buckling if ridden over a big pothole.

Hybrid or Trekking bikes: £150-£750

The Hybrid or Trekking bike is a mixture of the best elements of road and mountain bikes, and therefore very well suited to urban cyclists and leisure riders. They have larger diameter wheels, like road racing bikes, but slightly wider rims and tyres, making them stronger. They maintain good speed on the road and give the rider good control and stability. Like mountain bikes, they come equipped with lots of gears and have good brakes.

Some versions come with suspension that is designed for a more comfortable ride rather than control when riding on difficult terrain. The better versions also come with wide, comfortable, sprung saddles, often made with high-tech gel.

They have flat or riser handlebars that are curved upwards to give an upright riding posture. Sometimes they also have an adjustable handlebar stem so the rider can adjust the handlebar height to attain the most comfortable posture.

A few hybrids come fully equipped with mudguards, rear luggage rack and lights, which make them ideal for both leisure riding or regular commuting.

A new type of Hybrid is the Urban ATB, which, with smaller wheels, is closer to a mountain bike design than a road racing bike. They come with slick tyres for road riding, can be equipped with mudguards and they have better handling, but slightly less speed than an average hybrid.

Advantages When fully equipped, hybrids are perfect for commuting for the average rider. *Disadvantages* Not as fast as a road racing bike or as tough as a mountain bike.

Traditional Roadsters and City bikes £170-£600

These are the classic designed bikes that everybody rode in the 1950s (and that people still ride in Holland and Denmark).

They are typically steel-framed and are either single speed or have internal hub gears with 3-7 speeds. They are fully equipped with mudguards, chain cover, lights and rack, and sometimes even a dress-guard. They have riser handlebars which are slightly angled upwards, or have moustache handlebars which angle around like a moustache, giving a very upright riding position which is often referred to as 'sit-up-and-beg'. They come in both a ladies' frame design (with a low step-through frame for easy access and riding in a skirt) and a traditional gents' frame design with a high cross-bar.

Advantages The upright posture makes them comfortable to ride and gives you good visibility. The chain cover, mudguards and dress-guard protect everyday clothing. The more modern bikes of this design often come from Germany or Holland and can be quite light. The easy-to-use hub gears are adequate for most cities and require much less maintenance than derailleur gears. *Disadvantages* They can be heavy and slower than other bike designs.

Folding and compact bikes £150-£1,000

Folding bikes are perfect for commuters who come into the city by train, car or bus, as they can be folded up and taken on public transport.

The size of the wheels is anywhere from 12" to 26" – the smaller the wheels, the more compact the bike is when folded, but because of the size of the wheels they are less stable and the bike is not easy to ride fast. These bikes feel very nimble, but riding them can be tiring if you spend long periods in the saddle.

There are many designs of folding bike, some easier to fold than others. For a full breakdown and test ride of all the available versions, see the AtoB website or magazine, **www.atob.org.uk.**

Advantages Small and compact, they easily fit on public transport and have a small storage footprint. *Disadvantages* Less comfortable and slower to ride, they are also more expensive than a standard bike with the same parts specification.

Cruiser bikes £180-£500

Cruisers were developed in the States as big comfortable bikes with wide handlebars and big tyres; they have a laid-back riding posture for cruising down the boardwalks and cycle paths, along beaches and through parks. They are generally brightly coloured, with shiny mudguards and parts.

They were not designed for on-road riding, so their gears only have single, 3, 5 or 7 speeds, and they often do not have very good brakes – sometimes only a coaster brake on the back that works when you pedal backwards.

Recently they have had a surge of popularity in the UK and have been developed to be more suitable for road use.

Advantages They look stylish, and feel comfortable over short distances. *Disadvantages* The wide handlebars are not good for heavy traffic, and they are often heavy and slow.

Comfort Bike £250 – £600

Like cruiser bikes, comfort bikes were also developed in America for leisure cycling. The comfort bike is a mountain bike that has a more upright cycling posture. It is designed for light off-road cycling along forest tracks and bicycle paths.

Comfort bikes are fitted with comfortable grips, smooth-rolling semi-slick tyres, suspension on the front fork and seat-post, as well as a comfortable saddle. Like mountain bikes, they come with many gears and good brakes.

Advantages They are very comfortable and easy to ride, and versatile enough to ride in the city and for leisure. *Disadvantages* They are slower than a hybrid bicycle, and never come fully equipped with mudguards or rear rack.

Electric Bikes: £400 – £1,500

Electric bikes supplement the rider's pedal power with a battery-powered motor. A torque sensor detects how hard the rider is pushing on the pedals and supplements this by battery

power. Electric bikes can also come with a throttle like a motorbike, but all electric bikes are set to a maximum speed of 15 mph. They are very useful for hilly terrain, or for riders who do not want to strain themselves.

They come in all shapes and sizes, from electric mountain bikes to folding bikes. They have been on the market for over a decade, and although the original designs were heavy and unreliable, the technology has advanced in recent years and it is now possible to get a reliable, relatively low-cost bike with a fairly good range.

The key component is the battery; the best batteries are the lightest in weight and give the longest range.

- Lead acid batteries are the cheapest but also the heaviest, and will wear out the most quickly; they can be recharged up to 160 times.
- Nickel Metal Hydride (NiMH) batteries have good weight to power ratio and can be recharged up to 400 times.
- Lithium batteries are very lightweight and can usually be recharged over 1,000 times, but are very expensive.

For a full rundown of all the available models in the UK see the A to B website or magazine, www.atob.org.uk.

Advantages Perfect for older or less able cyclists who want a bit of a push, or for very hilly cities. *Disadvantages* They are heavier, more expensive, and cannot go any faster than 15 mph.

Bicycle Components

Although the components such as the gears, brakes, rims, hubs, frame and forks that are used to build your bike dictate the price, the relative advantages of all the various components could fill several books. Once you have decided what you need to use your bike for and how much you want to spend, if you get the right type of bike then the right components will be mostly chosen for you. That said, there are one or two parts that you should consider carefully when choosing your bike.

Parts and accessories like mudguards, lights and luggage carriers, although sometimes provided on a city bike, must often be bought separately (see Chapter 4, page 48).

Saddles

Riding with the wrong saddle may make your experience of cycling decidedly uncomfortable, so choosing the right saddle is one of the most important decisions you make when buying a bike. There are as many designs of saddle as there are bikes, using a variety of advanced gels and shapes to avoid discomfort. It is not always the case that a softer saddle will necessarily be more comfortable; many traditionalists swear by the classic sprung leather saddle which moulds itself to the shape of your posterior. Other cyclists prefer the cut-out designs that support the bones in your bottom but have a gap where pressure could cause discomfort.

Road racing bikes have very thin saddles which regular road bikers think are comfortable, although the main reason for this design is to save weight.

City cyclists are likely to find a broader saddle more comfortable, and ideally you want to rest the centre of your buttocks on the main part of the saddle. Bottoms come in all shapes and sizes, so before choosing a saddle for your bike it is recommended that you try it out first.

Suspension seat-posts
Many comfort and hybrid bikes are now fitted with a suspension seat-post, which is designed to absorb bumps from the road. They may make for a slightly more comfortable ride but are slightly heavier and can absorb energy from pedalling if not set up correctly.

Gears
The gears can be one of the most expensive parts of a bicycle, but, except in very hilly cities, you are very unlikely to need many gears. There are two types of gear system available: Derailleur and Hub.

Derailleur A derailleur leads the chain from one sprocket to another while the chain is moving forward. There are usually two derailleurs on a bike: one on the front with 3 gears, and another on the rear with between 5 and 9 gears, offering a total of up to 27 possible combinations.

Advantages It is usually lighter than a hub gear, and therefore used on most high-performance bikes. With all the parts on the outside, if something goes wrong with a derailleur system it is easier to reach and fix; it is also slightly easier to take the back wheel off to fix a puncture. *Disadvantages* A derailleur is a relatively high-maintenance system. As the chain is always shifting from one cog to another there is a lot of wear on the parts, and they are likely to need to be replaced after a few years of use. You will need to oil the chain on a regular basis and adjust the gear cables to keep it from slipping. It is also possible that the chain may fall off while riding.

Hub Gear Unlike the derailleur the hub gear has only one external cog and the speed is controlled through cogs inside the hub of the rear wheel. There are many fewer speeds, usually between 3 and 7, but the ratio between the highest and lowest gear is usually similar to a derailleur system.

Advantages A hub gear is relatively low maintenance, although you should still oil the chain and may need to adjust the cable length – although this will be required much less often, and the hub system should last for longer. The chain is less likely to fall off from a hub gear system and it is therefore recommended for city bikes. *Disadvantages* It is heavier, and if something does go wrong it is very hard to fix. It is also more difficult to remove the rear wheel.

Chapter 4

WHAT ELSE DO YOU NEED?

Once you have chosen the right bike there are still a few essential accessories you will need for cycling in a city, like a lock, some lights and a pump. The right clothing, a few parts such as mudguards and something to carry luggage will make your life more convenient and comfortable.

Clothing

You don't need any special clothing to ride a bike, and if you look at how the cyclists in Holland dress you will see that they mostly wear everyday clothing; a skirt-guard, fully enclosed chain, sensible sit-up-and-beg style bikes and a vastly superior cycle network make this possible. But if you plan to ride quickly through the British rush-hour traffic, or in the wet, then you should get some specialist cycling clothing to make you safer, more visible and more comfortable.

Gloves Your hands need protection. They will feel very cold in the winter, and if you fall off your bike and you are not wearing gloves you will definitely hurt your hands. There are gloves on the market with all sorts of gels and padding to absorb road vibrations, but any set of gloves is better than none. Remember that you still need good grip and control when you buy your winter gloves.

Helmets There is some debate about the pros and cons of wearing a helmet (there is no legal requirement to do so in this country); but if you land on your head it could save you from brain damage. If you plan to go fast or tackle any off-road sections, you should definitely wear a helmet. For more information see **www.whycycle.co.uk/safety-helmets.htm**.

When buying a helmet make sure you get the right size, and fit it correctly. Buy the smallest helmet that is comfortable, to ensure it fits tightly on your head. Tighten the straps so that they feel tight when you have your mouth open. When trying your helmet on, remember that it is worn on top of the head, not tipped back.

High-visibility vest / brownie belt To make sure that car drivers see you, wearing a high-visibility vest or reflective straps (brownie belt) makes sense when riding in a city. A few years ago a high-visibility vest would have seemed 'uncool'; these days, at least in London where  cycling has become hugely popular, they could almost be considered a fashion accessory. You can get them from cycle or hardware shops (as most workmen are now required to wear high-visibility clothing, you can also sometimes find them discarded on a building site). These days you can choose from a variety of different colours or designs, but with a can of spray paint, some scissors, cardboard, masking tape and a bit of creativity, you can join the uber-cool and customise your vest with your own Banksy-style graffiti. Some of the most artistic riders at the London Critical Mass (see page 90) appear to have cut the reflective strips off a vest and sewn it in pretty patterns onto their ordinary jackets.

Specialist cycle clothing There is specialist clothing on the market which is designed to wick the sweat from your body to keep you cool in the summer and warm in the winter. Although not necessary for a leisurely commute, good-quality cycle clothing can make life much more comfortable on longer journeys. Mountain biking gear has the same performance as tight-fitting road biking gear, but is more baggy and may be more suited to those with less athletic bodies.

Shorts In the summer it is nice to change into shorts to ride, and cycle shorts come with a padded bottom that makes for a slightly more comfortable ride. You can buy baggy mountain biking shorts if you are not a fan of Lycra.

Waterproofs Cycle capes are the traditional way to ride in the rain and are great value, very efficient, and ideal if you get caught in the rain. They don't perform well in wind, however, so if you want to speed to work in all weathers, breathable, lightweight waterproof jackets and trousers are best. Priced from as little as £50, a good set will keep you pretty dry even in a major storm and can make riding in the rain seem almost fun. Traditional waterproof footwear or waterproof boots which fit over your shoes will keep your feet dry, although a couple of plastic bags held on by elastic bands will suffice in an emergency.

Keeping your head dry can be more difficult, and it is important not to obscure your visibility so don't use a hood. You can get helmet covers or, if you prefer to ride without a helmet, a baseball hat with a peak; although not waterproof, this will keep the rain off your head and out of your eyes.

Chain Guard Getting clothes caught in the chain can tear them or make them oily – a chain guard avoids this. Dutch bikes come with a completely enclosed chain, but the standard half guards that are fitted to many hybrid bikes are also good. Cycle clips are cheap and effective for keeping your trousers away from the chain.

Lights

By law, if you ride in the dark you must have front, rear, wheel and pedal reflectors, which should come ready-fitted on a new bike; you also need a white front and a red rear light. Cycling at night without lights is not only dangerous, it could cost you a £30 fine for each missing light. There are three main types of light:

Dynamo These are often pre-fitted on a fully equipped commuter's bike. They gain power from the turning wheels and do not require batteries. Prices vary, but a good set of dynamos will start at about £50. However, they go out when you stop and make the bike a bit harder to pedal.

LED (light-emitting diodes) Modern LEDs are very powerful, lightweight and have a long battery life. Prices start at £6 for a set of two.

Halogen These give a strong beam of light so you can both see and be seen – particularly useful if you are riding on unlit roads. Their main disadvantage is the battery life; you will typically only get a couple hours use from alkaline batteries. You can get a rechargeable battery pack from around £40.

Locks and security

Having your bike stolen is pretty annoying, and protecting it from thieves is as much about choosing the right place to leave it as what lock you have. Compact folding bikes can be carried into the shop, office, or home; the problem is that it is not always convenient or possible to carry one around all the time. Most workplaces and schools now have cycle parking, which is also available in most city centres. A very public place, ideally with CCTV, will be the most secure. An old-looking bike (even if is actually valuable and new) is also a good bet, and you can cover your bike in electrical tape or paint, which will disguise the brand from a prospective thief.

No matter where you lock it, what lock you use, or how old and battered your bike looks, there is a chance that you will have your bike stolen. In order to trace it, it is worth recording the unique identity number which is stamped on every frame, usually on the underside of the bottom bracket. You should also record the model and make, and take a picture. For expensive bikes, you can also have a micro-dot embedded in the frame; this is registered with the police, so you stand a better chance of getting it back if stolen.

When locking your bike outside you should remember to also protect your wheels and seat-post; quick-release bolts make adjusting the seat height or taking the wheels off very easy, but also offer easy pickings. If you sometimes leave your bike outside cinemas and shops, it is probably worth swapping the quick-releases for conventional nuts and bolts. Otherwise, when you lock the bike be sure to lock the wheels to the frame and take the saddle with you.

A good cycle lock is essential if you are going to leave your bike outside unattended; a modern-looking bike is more likely to be stolen than an old one. Thieves will take anything, so you should definitely buy a lock when you buy the bike, even if it is an old second-hand relic. Any lock can be broken by a professional thief, but as most bikes are stolen by opportunists using garage tools, the stronger the lock the less likely it is that your bike will be stolen.

There are hundreds of different locks on the market, ranging in price from £2 to £100, but as with most things, you get what you pay for. A good guide to what lock to buy can be found at Sold Secure, **www.soldsecure.com**.

Sold Secure 'Gold'-rated locks offer maximum security but are expensive and may be too bulky to carry easily, while 'Silver' and 'Bronze' levels should provide adequate protection. A simple way to decide what lock you need is to think where you will be leaving your bike, how long it will be unattended, and how much it is worth. Rather than carry a heavy expensive lock around with you, why not lock it where you park your bike (assuming you don't need it at the other end!)? All you need to carry then is your keys, which are much lighter.

Cable locks Coil and cable locks are easy to carry, can be looped round the bike and are very flexible. Ideally you should choose a cable long enough to lock the wheels to the frame and to a cycle stand. Although very convenient, only very thick and strong cables are resistant to standard bolt cutters.

Chains Good thick chains and padlocks can be very heavy to carry, but the chain can be as long as you like. This is a good option if you lock your bike in high-risk areas for long periods.

D-Locks Heavy steel D-Locks are strong and resistant to most bolt cutters, but can be harder to carry. They also do not have any flexibility, so it can be more difficult to find somewhere to lock the bike. Double-security locks provide both the security of a D-Lock and have a long cable so you can still lock both wheels.

If you have an expensive bike and need to lock it outside, you can disguise it to deter thieves. Try wrapping the frame in tape or use paint to make it look old and ugly.

Luggage carriers

Carrying luggage on a bike is simple, whether it is your laptop, paperwork or smart clothes.

Backpacks Backpacks will make your back sweat, so are not ideal when you are wearing your work clothes, However they can be fitted with a laptop insert and are good for carrying both your laptop and work clothes if you don't have panniers.

Briefcase pannier This is designed to fix onto the luggage rack, and looks smart and professional when carried by hand; a briefcase pannier fits a standard laptop, and usually has room for clean clothes and some papers.

Basket and handlebar bags These hook onto the handlebar and are a convenient way to carry small loads. Classic ladies' bikes are usually fitted with a basket, and are very convenient for holding a few items if you are using your bike around town. Wicker or metal are both available, and men can also buy more 'masculine' designs based on Post Office bikes.

Standard panniers One single-side pannier offers plenty of space to cram in most things you could want at work, and you can get fully waterproof designs, pannier covers or waterproof inserts to keep your clothes dry if it rains.

Wedge bags that fit under the seat are a great way to carry the essential tools for emergency repairs.

Trailers Trailers are the best way to carry really large or heavy loads. The main disadvantage is that a trailer increases the length of the bike, making it more difficult to control and ride in a city.

Rear luggage rack If you want to carry panniers, then you will need a luggage rack: you should choose one that has two or three legs that provide wide side support for the load. Welded luggage racks that are the strongest, followed by bolted racks; the type that clamps onto the seat-post is the weakest. Once you have a rack you should also buy some bungee cords or cargo net to hold down the odd load like waterproofs (or your jacket if it gets too hot etc.).

Mudguards

Without mudguards, the spray from your wheels on a wet road will splash all over you. Modern mudguards are made of advanced plastics that are light and almost unbreakable. Prices start at around £20 for a set.

There are two types: full-wheel and quick-fix. Full-wheel are recommended if they fit your bike, as they catch all the road spray, while quick-fix are suitable for mountain bikes which often cannot take standard mudguards.

Tools

A pump, a multi-tool and a puncture repair kit can all be carried with you – see Chapter 6, pages 59-60 for more information.

Chapter Five

GETTING STARTED

As the old phrase goes, "It's like riding a bike": once you learn you never forget, and despite the decline of cycle use in the UK, most of us had bikes as children and can still ride one. Is there anything that adults need to learn about riding a bike?

There are more cars on the road than ever before, and surveys show that the biggest barrier to the take-up of cycling is the perception of danger. Confident cyclists who have good road position and excellent control of their bikes are the safest. If it has been several years since you were last on a bike, and the prospect of cycling on a busy road is daunting, then a few hours on a training course (many are free, or subsidised) will do wonders for your confidence and safety – and they are good fun. See the listings at the end of this chapter for information on cycle trainers in your area.

Before you ride on the road

Before jumping on the bike and launching yourself onto the open road, here are a few tips:

Have a roadworthy bike A bike bought from a bike shop should be ready to ride. If you already have a bike, seek the advice of a mechanic at a bicycle shop or use the checklist below:

- **Brakes** Look to see if the brake pads look worn. Lift the front wheel, spin and pull the front brake: the wheel should immediately stop turning. Repeat with the rear wheel.
- **Tyres** Test with thumb to see that the tyres are firm, if not pump them up.

- **Wheels** Check that the wheels are true: lift the front wheel and spin it to make sure it is not impeded, and repeat with rear wheel. Check that the wheels are clamped securely.
- **Handlebars** Hold the front wheel between your legs and wiggle the handlebars to ensure they are tight and aligned correctly.
- **Saddle height** You should be able to sit in the saddle and touch the ground with your toes.
- **Test-ride** Before venturing onto a road, the final check should be a test-ride. Find a safe, car-free area and take a ride, operating the brakes and gears, and making sure the bike is comfortable. Do not ignore strange noises or jumping gears, as they probably indicate a problem.

Bicycle maintenance is covered in Chapter 6, but if you have any doubts about the mechanical safety of your bicycle, seek help from your local bike shop.

If you have never ridden a bike before, consider starting with a ladies' bike with a low, step-through frame. Stand with legs astride the bike, hold the handlebars, put one foot on a pedal, push forward with the other foot and start pedalling. You may wobble a bit at first, but the faster you go the less you will wobble.

Steering To get used to steering your bike, try practising manoeuvering between some obstacles, and making u-turns.

Signalling and communication Probably the most important part of riding on the road is good communication with other road users. Before you take to the road you should practise riding with one hand, and looking behind whilst signalling. Before you manoeuvre, make sure there are no obstacles in front, and then look behind you and try to make eye contact with the approaching car drivers. Always clearly signal what you are going to do.

Braking There are two brakes on a bike, front and back; the back brake is usually operated by the left hand and the front brake by the right hand. Both levers are on the handlebars. These are the most important part of the bike, so get used to the brake set-up and operating it.

Practise in a car-free area, and get used to riding with your fingers on the brake levers. If this is very uncomfortable, or if you find the brakes are not working well, seek the advice of a mechanic at a bike shop.

Use the back brake to slow down, and both front and back brakes together to stop.

Emergency Stops To stop quickly, simultaneously pull hard on the back and front brakes, shift your weight backwards, moving your posterior towards the back of the saddle while stiffening your arms. It sounds more difficult than it is; practise a few times.

- **Avoid skidding** Pulling the back brake hard will lock the rear wheel, which will cause you to skid. Like ABS in cars, brakes work most effectively when the wheels are still turning. If you start to skid, release the brake lever slightly.
- **Do not pull the front brake on its own suddenly** as this could throw you over the handlebars. When using the front brake, shift your weight towards the back of the bike.
- **Never turn the handlebar while pulling hard on the front brake** – the front wheel will skid, and you could lose control.

Operating the Gears Many bikes have gears, which make it both easier to climb hills and get high speeds on the flat. Unless you live in a very hilly area you are unlikely to need more than a few gears for everyday use. Most gears are controlled from the handlebar either as a twist-grip, as quick-fire (buttons that are pressed by thumb and forefinger), or incorporated into the brake levers.

There are two main types of gears – derailleur and hub – which are operated differently. Each has advantages and disadvantages (see Chapter 3, pages 38-39).

With **derailleur** gears, you change gear whilst pedalling forwards. The front derailleur is controlled from the left side shifter, the rear derailleur from the right shifter. Different gear speeds are achieved from combinations of the front and rear derailleurs.

On the front, the largest sprocket is the highest gear, while on the back the smallest is the highest gear. A 27-speed bike will have 3 speeds on the front and 9 on the rear, giving 27 possible combinations. However, try to avoid the gears that make the chain cross over at an extreme angle; these "criss-cross" gears are bad for the chain and sprockets. Especially bad is to combine the inside (small) front sprocket with the outside (small) rear sprocket; this combination is noisy, inefficient, and causes the chain to wear out prematurely.

With **hub** gears you briefly stop pedalling to change gear. A hub gear only has one external cog, and the speed is controlled through cogs inside the hub of the wheel. There are fewer gears, usually between 3 and 7, but this system is easier to operate and the ratio between the highest and lowest gear is usually the same as a 27-speed derailleur system.

Be visible

Before you join the traffic you should ensure that you are visible: wear a high-visibility jacket and have lights on your bike if you might be cycling in the dark.

On the road

Once you have learned to control your bike, and are confident with turning, braking and changing gears, you are ready to cycle on the road, but before you do you should be aware of the basics of road position.

There are two main positions for on-road cycling. You can ride in the traffic stream (the primary position) or to the left of it (the secondary position).

Primary Position If riding in the middle of a lane you are part of the traffic, and are very visible to drivers because you are right in front of them. This position should be adopted in residential streets, especially when parked cars on either side may mean there is not enough room for safe overtaking. You are also doing drivers a favour by removing the decision from them as to whether or not there is room to squeeze past you.

Secondary Position Riding to the left of the traffic stream, in the secondary position, is a concession to road users coming from behind at higher speeds, allowing them to pass. This position is usually adopted on main roads.

The distance from the kerb depends on the width of the road, but as a rule of thumb leave at least one metre between yourself and the kerb.

Inexperienced cyclists often ride too close to the kerb. This is dangerous, as if you hit a bump, or a car door opens, or a pedestrian or pet runs out in front of you, you can only swerve into the traffic stream. But if you are further away from the kerb and someone overtaking gets too close, you still have room to move back towards the left. Generally, cars will give you as much room as you give yourself.

Passing parked cars When passing parked cars, always be aware that a car door could open, so look to see if the cars are occupied.

Taking the lane There are occasions where you should move from the secondary to the primary position. This is called 'taking the lane'.

Places where you should take the lane include:

- passing parked cars
- approaching and moving through a junction
- riding in a bus lane
- moving through a narrowing road

– in fact whenever you want to ensure you are not overtaken. To do so, plan well ahead, look over your right shoulder to see if it is clear. If it is clear far enough behind so that no one will be affected, move right into the traffic stream. You may have to wait. Good communication and signalling should enable you to negotiate your way into the traffic stream.

Junctions Approaching traffic lights or a junction where you must give way, position yourself in the primary position in the centre of the lane. If when approaching a junction there is a queue of traffic, the least safe option is to undertake on the left, so be very cautious and never undertake a lorry or large vehicle. It is best to either wait your turn or consider overtaking (on the right) to get to the front, where there is often a reserved area for cyclists.

Clearly signal your right or left turn, and look behind to check the drivers are giving way. Then when it is clear, or the lights are green, cycle through the junction maintaining your primary position in the centre of the lane.

Roundabouts Roundabouts are the most dangerous places for inexperienced cyclists. To be safe, it is very important to signal clearly and maintain communication with other road users. At a roundabout, as visibility is all-important, you should arrive at, and move through in the middle of the most appropriate lane. Look all around you and signal your intentions clearly.

Chapter 6

CYCLE MAINTENANCE FOR BEGINNERS

Keeping your bike on the road

Part of the beauty of bicycle design is its simplicity, which means that the common repair jobs are not difficult to do yourself. If you have an absolute aversion to getting your hands dirty, however, in most towns and cities there are plenty of cycle shops where a mechanic will happily fix anything from a puncture to a bottom bracket at relatively low cost. Be aware that expensive performance bikes are likely to require more maintenance than city bikes.

Most cycle shops also provide servicing, and since keeping your bike well maintained will ensure it works better and lasts longer, taking it for a regular service will probably save you money. If you completely disregard cycle maintenance you are more likely to encounter mechanical problems that will be difficult and expensive to fix.

Only the very basics of cycle maintenance are covered here, but if you aspire to be a trained mechanic there are courses you can take and plenty of further reading you can do.

The Essential Tools

The following tools are recommended for basic bicycle maintenance.

- *Cycle oil* You must keep your chain well oiled, and for the minimum trouble, traditional cycle oil, also known as wet lube, is ideal. It will stay on your chain even in the wet and keep your chain lubricated for a relatively long time. Dry lube, often with an additive like PTFE or Teflon, will lubricate your chain and has the advantage of keeping it clean, preventing the build-up of dirt. It washes off in the wet, however, so you will need to regularly reapply it.

- *Latex gloves and a rag* Bicycles get dirty, you will need an old rag to wipe off excess oil. As you probably don't want to get filthy hands, a pair of latex gloves, although not essential, are a very useful part of a tool kit.

- *Multi-tool* Individual tools will be easier to use, but a multi-tool comes in an easy to carry package and has most of the tools you need for basic bicycle maintenance. There are many versions on the market, but ideally a multi-tool should have at least an allen key set, flat and Phillips screw drivers, and a set of spanners.

- *Pump* Tyres lose pressure over time, and when they do they have greater rolling resistance. Pumping up your tyres is quicker and easier with a big chamber floor pump which you can keep at home, and a mini-pump which is easily carried on the bike.

- *Puncture repair kit* A puncture repair kit should include tyre levers, patches and rubber solution. New self-adhesive patches are now also available, and are easier to use, but more expensive.

The absolute basics

Even if you suffer from chronic mechanical incompetence and were almost entering high school before you learned to tie your shoe laces, there are a couple of very easy jobs that you should be able to do yourself to keep your bike in good working order.

Lubricating your chain If you start to hear squeaky noises from your chain when you ride, then it needs lubrication; if you continue to ride with a dry chain, more expensive parts will wear out very quickly. To lube the chain, simply apply cycle oil to the entire length of the chain as you turn the pedal backwards, being careful not to allow oil to leak onto the rim of the rear wheel which will affect your braking. It is best to clean your chain before oiling: specialist de-greasers can be bought from a cycle shop.

Pumping up the tyres You will need to pump them up a little bit about once a month. There are two common bicycle tube valves: Presta and Schrader – check which type your bike has. Most pumps can be set to inflate either valve type, so simply adjust your pump to the correct valve setting and inflate the tyres until they feel solid when pressed with your thumb. It is possible to over-inflate with a floor pump, so stop pumping when the tyre feels feel hard. If your pump has a pressure gauge, inflate to the recommended pressures stamped on the side wall of the tyre.

Presta valve   *Schrader valve*

Common repairs

Punctures

There is no more annoying or common problem than a puncture, so the best advice is to be careful where you ride: avoid areas where the hedges have been newly cut, or where there is glass on the road.

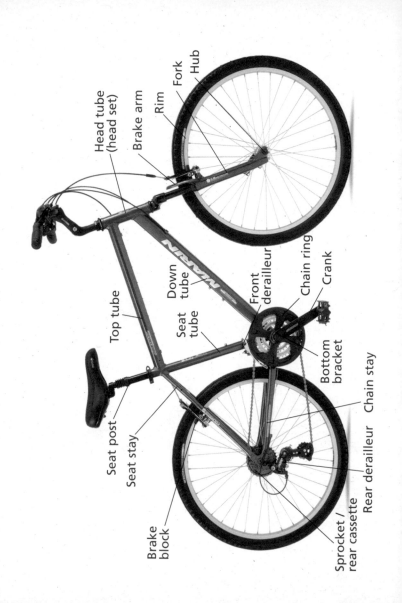

Head tube (head set)

Brake arm

Rim

Fork

Hub

Top tube

Down tube

Front derailleur

Chain ring

Crank

Seat tube

Bottom bracket

Seat post

Seat stay

Chain stay

Brake block

Sprocket / rear cassette

Rear derailleur

Buy a bike fitted with puncture-resistant tyres or fit them yourself. There are many types available. You can also buy a puncture-resistant strip and line your tyres yourself. There are inner tubes available that are filled with puncture-resistant goo – the best known is 'Slime', which reacts with air to automatically seal a puncture if you get one. No prevention system is foolproof, and when you hear the inevitable hiss of escaping air you should stop riding and either repair it yourself or push it to the nearest cycle shop.

Fixing punctures If you have quick-release wheels, it is usually easier to remove the wheel to work on a puncture, although it should be possible to fix the puncture while the wheel is still on.

1. Release the brakes You will need to release your brakes to get access to the tube or to remove the wheel.

V-brakes: Press the top of the two brake arms together and disengage the cable to allow the arms to spring apart.

Other Brakes: Road bikes and some folding bikes have side-pull brakes. These often have a switch that releases the brake blocks from the wheel, or you may have to remove one of the brake blocks with an allen key. When you buy a bike, ask for instructions on how to release the brakes so that you can remove the wheel.

2. Remove the wheel After releasing the brakes you can remove the wheel. If you have quick-release skewers, you simply open the quick-release lever and take the wheel off, twisting the nut slightly to open it wider if the wheel will not come off easily. If removing the rear wheel you will need to take it off the chain, which will be much easier if the chain is on the smallest outside cog in top gear.

If you do not have quick-release wheels you will need the right sized spanner to loosen the axle nuts, but otherwise the process is the same.

If you have hub gears, you will need to unscrew the cable brake in order to remove the wheel.

3. Check the tyre visually to see if you can spot where the tyre has been holed; run your hand along the tyre to feel for a sharp object, which if found should be removed. Make a mental note of the position of the puncture on the wheel if you can find it.

4. Remove the tube Ideally take three tyre levers, wedge them under the tyre and pull it up and over the wheel rim, using the spokes to fix them in place. Be careful not to catch the inner tube with the lever, or you might cause another puncture.

Take another tyre lever and use it to lever the tyre off the rim, a centimetre or two along from the first lever, to widen the gap. Continue to widen the gap in this way using the third lever, until it is possible to run a lever around the rim to fully remove one side of the tyre.

Remove the valve cap and threaded metal collar if there is one, and empty the tube of any remaining air. Push the valve back through the hole in the rim, and carefully pull the tube out from under the tyre.

5. Find the hole Once out, inflate the inner tube and listen or feel for the escaping air; if you have water handy, you can submerge the tube in water and watch for bubbles.

6. Apply a patch With a traditional puncture repair kit, clean the area around the hole then dry it, put a dab of rubber solution on the hole, and using your finger, gently spread it in a small circular area around the hole. Wait for the solution to dry, apply the patch and push hard to make sure there are no air bubbles. When you are happy the patch is secure, you can grate some chalk on the area to prevent the inner tube sticking to the tyre when it is replaced. If you have self-adhesive patches, you only need to find the puncture, clean and rough the tube, before applying the patch.

7. Check for more holes Re-inflate the inner tube and check its entire length for more holes.

8. Check for sharp objects Before you put the tube back, you must ensure the sharp object that caused the puncture has been removed. Use a finger to feel along the whole of the inside of the tyre, checking the area where the inner tube was punctured particularly carefully.

9. Replace the tube Remove all air from the tube, place the valve back into the rim, and work the tube back under the tyre onto the wheel. Hook the tyre back onto the rim with your hands; you may need to use a tyre lever to hook the last section back onto the tyre. Be very careful not to pinch the tube between the tyre and rim, as this could cause another puncture. Replace the threaded collar and pump up the tyre.

Cables

Cables are used on bicycles for operating the brakes and gears. Cables stretch and sometimes snap, and occasionally need tightening and replacing. Cable stretch is particularly pronounced when the cables are new; because of this, most bicycle shops will give a free service two weeks after you buy a new bike.

Tightening your brake cable If you can pull the brake lever until it almost touches the handlebar grip, then you need to tighten the cable.

Small adjustments can be made with threaded adjusters, which are usually found either where the cable comes out of the brake lever, or sometimes where the cable goes into the brakes. Simply unscrew this to extend the cable until your brakes feel tighter. After making an adjustment, twist the threaded outer locking nut back to the brake lever to lock the new position in place.

For bigger adjustments, follow the cable down from the brake lever to the other end, where you will see it is locked in place with a clamp bolt. Loosen this nut, using an allen key or nut wrench, to allow the cable to move freely. Pull the cable through with your fingers or pliers until the brake blocks are positioned just a couple of millimetres on either side of the rim; then securely tighten the clamp bolt.

Clamping bolt

After adjusting the brakes, always check that the wheel turns freely and that the brakes work well before riding again.

Tightening your gear cable Derailleur gear cables occasionally stretch, which will make your shifting inaccurate. Small adjustments can be made with twist adjusters where the cable comes out of the shifter on the handlebars. Simply turn the adjuster one or two revolutions to tighten the cable slightly, and continue to turn until the gears are back in sync.

To make further adjustments, turn the bike upside down and you will see another adjuster where the cable goes into the gears by the rear wheel. Turn this adjuster a revolution or two. To check if the gears are in sync, simply turn the pedals while the bike is upturned and shift through the gears.

Adjuster   Clamping bolt

For bigger adjustments, put the bike into top gear, loosen the clamping bolt and pull the cable through while pushing the derailleur in slightly with your hand. Tighten the clamping bolt and check again to see if the gears are in sync.

Replacing a brake cable Cables not only stretch but they can snap if not maintained properly. This happens most often with brake cables; if it does, you should stop riding immediately. You will also need to replace the cable if the cable housing becomes frayed or bent, as it will make the cable stick. Regularly check for frayed cables and cable housing.

To replace a cable you will also need cable cutters or a hacksaw, and tiny cable caps to put on the end of the cable to prevent it fraying.

1. Undo the cable at the far end by loosening the clamping bolt.

2. As you remove the old cable, place the parts in a line so that you can easily see where everything goes. Even if you're planning to replace the housing, keep the old sections so you can cut the new pieces to match.

3. With the cable loose, pull the lever all the way back to the handlebar; this will expose a hole that contains a knob on the end of the cable. Line this knob up with the hole and push it out.

4. When released, pull the cable out from the brake lever end.

5. If replacing the cable housing get the cable cutters or a hack saw to cut the pieces the same size as those you have removed.

6. Insert the new cable through the brake lever, ensuring that the round knob at the cable end is fitted securely back into the hole. Then begin assembling the sections of cable housing onto the cable. If you are replacing cable housing you will need to fit a metal cap or cable stop onto every end. Fit the housing into the mountings at the brake lever, and at each mounting of the frame.

7. Pull the cable back through to the clamping bolt, adjust the brakes to the correct position and tighten the clamping bolt to secure. Check that the brakes now work properly and adjust the position if necessary.

8. Use the cable cutters to cut off excess cable, take a cable cap and place on the end of the cable and use pliers to compress the cable cap so it stays on the end.

Replacing brake blocks

With regular use, brakes blocks will require replacing. If the brakes are tight but still do not work very well, then you probably need to replace the brake blocks; never allow them to wear through to the metal, as this will quickly destroy your wheel rims which are expensive to replace, while a set of brake blocks can be bought for just a few pounds.

When replacing with the new blocks, be sure that they are aligned properly with the wheel rim. After they are tightened, pull the brake to check that they do not rub against the tyre, as this will cause a puncture.

Cleaning your bike

To keep your bike in good working order and prolong its life, give it a good clean once in a while. There are several cleaning fluids on the market that when diluted and sprayed on the bike will cut through the dirt and oil to make this job easier. After cleaning, do not forget to re-oil the chain. There are many eco-friendly bike cleaners on the market.

More difficult repairs

Replacing gear cables, adjusting your gears, straightening buckled wheels or replacing a spoke are all repair jobs that you can also learn to do yourself and are worthwhile if you plan to take your bike on a long adventure; however, they require a degree of skill. For the beginner is it is much easier to take your bike to the local bike shop and have it repaired by a professional.

Several cycling and sustainable transport websites (such as Sustrans) give information about maintenance: see pages 89-93.

Chapter 7

IS YOUR WORKPLACE CYCLE-FRIENDLY?

Ten years ago it was hard to find even a single cycle parking stand at an office. Nowadays, realising that a parking space costs up to £2,000 a year to maintain, many workplaces have installed secure cycle shelters. Some have state-of-the-art changing rooms, and a few even provide cash incentives to encourage their staff to cycle to work instead of driving, as part of their organisation's Travel Plan. Travel Plans were introduced to the UK in 1997 from the USA, where they are used as part of the solution for the air pollution problems in California. A Travel Plan is a package of measures to promote car sharing, car clubs, public transport use and walking and cycling.

Today, new developments, both residential and commercial, normally have a Travel Plan to offset the impact of the extra traffic they generate, as part of the planning application. Local authorities are keen to encourage cycling as a means of reducing congestion, and have installed cycle parking in most town centres. They work with employers to encourage them to promote sustainable transport to their staff through adopting a Travel Plan.

Even though great progress has been made towards making more places cycle-friendly, many workplaces still have no facilities for cyclists. Even where organisations are working to promote cycling, their effectiveness depends on the participation of the staff and visitors.

WILTSHIRE COUNTY COUNCIL

Wiltshire County Council, in support of its Travel Plan and corporate objective to become the healthiest county in Britain by 2014, has introduced numerous incentives for staff to encourage them to cycle, including brand new covered and secure cycle parking, 10 minutes "changing time" granted as part of core flexi-time, new personal lockers throughout its campus, as well as upgrading a set of ladies 'and gents' shower rooms to rival any private leisure club.

And whilst staff are at work, the benefits for cycling on business have also been addressed with a 40p per mile business bike rate and three pool bikes available, including a ladies' and gents' mountain bike, a Brompton folding bike – ideal to take on the train via the station two minutes cycle away – and a trailer. As a key part of National Bike Week events, the county council also organises evening staff cycle rides straight after work to pubs via the Kennett and Avon Canal path. A little gentle lubrication of the legs for would-be cyclists and know-how tips from regular cyclists is vital to encourage more staff to take up the habit.

Cycle parking

Having a secure place to leave your bicycle is essential, although it is often possible to lock bicycles to railings or lamp-posts. However this looks untidy, is in full view of potential thieves, provides no protection from the elements – and the popular places are often full. Organisations that fit good quality cycle parking send a message to staff and visitors that cycling is valued.

There is a wide variety of cycle parks available, from a simple covered cycle shed to impressive futuristic designs. For small offices or apartments, however, a simple hook or wall attachment can be fitted from as little as £50. Where possible, cycle parking should be placed in a secure location to discourage thieves, either in clear view of the office, or as part of an underground car park if there is one.

It is just as important to have somewhere safe to park your bike at home. If you lack space, then there are cycle storage solutions that hang from a wall, but if you live in an apartment or terraced house with no room to store a bicycle inside, a wall hook and a strong lock should keep the bicycle secure outside. In an apartment building it is a good idea to first approach the residents' committee and suggest they fit some cycle parking.

Showers and changing rooms

It is nice to be able to change and shower before you start work. Providing high quality facilities for cyclists is a clear signal that the employer values staff who choose to cycle instead of driving, and when car parking costs so much to maintain, it makes good business sense.

Consequently many large employers have fitted extensive changing rooms for cyclists, close to the cycle parking. These include lockers, showers and even ironing boards. Employers should take care when allocating lockers that there is a system in place to ensure they are in regular use. There have been cases when lockers are still allocated to staff who don't cycle regularly or who have even left the company.

For small businesses without the budget for such extensive facilities, just the addition of a shower in the toilets is sufficient to cater for the needs of an employee who wishes to cycle to work.

GLAXOSMITHKLINE, LONDON

GSK's head office on the West Road in Brentford, London has 3,500 staff but only 1,500 parking spaces, so access to these rare spaces is rotated amongst the staff.

Led by Peter Handcock, the Vice President of Global Real Estate who is a keen cyclist, they have developed one of the best cycle promotion schemes in the country.

Cyclists are treated to secure cycle parking located in the buildings' underground car park. Next to the cycle park are changing rooms that feature all the mod cons a cyclist could need; ample storage in generous-sized lockers, coat hangers with integrated locks, showers, hair dryers, and even an iron.

To encourage more staff to cycle, they can register on the GSK bike miles scheme. Staff receive a bike miles card and sticker booklet, and each day they enter the site on a bicycle they are given a bike miles sticker. Once they have filled the first 50 stickers in the booklet they can exchange it for cycling goodies to the value of £50 from one of the partner bicycle stores. They can also use their tokens to employ the services of Dr. Bike, a local mechanic who is on site twice a week and is available to do maintenance and repairs.

Bicycle user groups (BUGs)

In many large organisations bicycle user groups are formed to discuss anything from cycle maintenance to the best routes to and from the office. They are also excellent ways to meet fellow cyclists who may cycle in a similar direction and might be interested in becoming cycle buddies, cycling to and from work together. Ask in the office if there is an existing BUG; if not you can form one with just a few posters or an email to everyone on the intranet.

PFIZER: SANDWICH, KENT

Pharmaceutical giant Pfizer chose the Kent coast to build their European manufacturing plant. Pfizer's Director of Manufacturing, John Gough, is a keen cyclist and champions his company's commitment to maintain excellent provision for cyclists.

Concerned that the historic town of Sandwich would be swamped by an influx of 3,000 cars, the company was encouraged to promote alternatives to single-occupant-car commuting, and one of the first UK travel plans was born.

Besides running private bus services linking the plant to the nearby station and Canterbury, and an effective car share scheme, Pfizer invested in cycle lanes that link the site to the wonderful coastline National Cycle Network route that runs down from Ramsgate and along to Deal. This stretch of the NCN is well used by tourists at the weekends, and many Pfizer employees get to ride it every day for their daily commute. On-site there are changing rooms and secure bike parking, and employees receive a daily £2 bonus for not using their car.

Incentives to ride

As mentioned in Chapter 1, a healthy workforce is more productive and has fewer days absent, and regular cycling is one of the best ways to get and stay healthy. Cyclists are statistically the most punctual employees and a bicycle takes up a lot less parking space, saving employers money. These advantages have meant some employers even offer their staff incentives to get out of the car and onto a bicycle.

Incentives vary from a 'bike miles' token card, which is stamped every time the employee arrives by bicycle and when full can be redeemed against free cycling gear, to a free biker's breakfast once a month.

Salary sacrifice schemes

The government started a scheme a few years ago whereby employees can buy a bike through their employer at up to 50% discount off the retail price. The money is taken directly from the employee's gross salary, saving on income tax, VAT and national insurance.

There are companies that will help an employer set up a salary sacrifice scheme, which can even be implemented at very small companies. Check with your HR department if your company has a scheme, and if not suggest they check out the information from: www.bikeforall.net/content/cycle_to_work_scheme.php.

Pool bikes

Many workplaces are on industrial estates that are a few miles from the centre of town, which means employees drive to work so they have access to a car for lunch breaks or local meetings. Some organisations therefore provide a few pool bikes, which any member of staff can borrow for a few hours to pop to a local meeting or to get something for lunch.

City-based organisations find that the provision of a few pool bikes can significantly reduce taxi use and save the company money.

Bike servicing

The provision of once-monthly on-site bike servicing by a bike mechanic from a local bicycle store is also a great way to encourage staff to cycle, and is important if the company has pool bikes.

ARBURY ROAD VETERINARY CLINIC, CAMBRIDGE

Arbury Road Veterinary Clinic is a small company with less than 10 employees in a busy area of Cambridge – which itself is very congested.

They have fitted cycle parking which was funded through Take A Stand scheme run by Cambridgeshire Travel To Work Partnership. They have introduced a Bike-To-Work tax-free scheme for staff to get lower cost bikes and accessories, have fitted an on-site shower, and pay staff a £1 a day bonus for arriving at work by any means other than car. These measures have had results: the percentage of staff arriving by private car is now below 30%, down from 77% in 2005.

BikeWeek / Bike2Work

Once a year in the third week of June there is a nationally coordinated week of bike events. It is an opportunity for employers to get as many staff as possible to try cycling. Anyone can organise a Bike Week event: this could be a prize draw, bike competition, biker breakfast, free bike servicing, lunchtime or evening leisure ride, or anything that you imagine would be an effective way to get people to give cycling a try. BikeWeek will provide organisers with free gifts and promotional materials.

Cycle Training

Employers that wish to encourage their staff to cycle often organize free cycle training to encourage less confident cyclists to give it a try.

Chapter 8

IT'S NOT ALL WORK

Cycling is not just a great way to get to work – it is also a great way to spend your free time. Whether it is taking the family on a ride along a cycle path, joining a bike club to ride at speed on a road bike, performing death-defying stunts on a BMX, crossing the Alps on a bike adventure, or charging down a gnarly track on a mountain bike, cycling can be a lot of fun. All of us can remember the excitement of riding a bike as a child, and if it's been a while since you were last on a bike, you'll probably be surprised that it can be just as exciting as an adult.

Leisure cycling

The National Cycle Network (NCN), constructed by the cycle charity Sustrans, is a UK-wide network of over 10,000 miles of cycle lanes which passes within a mile of over half of the UK population. Many sections of the network are car-free and run through pleasant and often beautiful landscapes. The NCN can be easily accessed either by starting cycling from home, or by taking the bikes on a train or on the back of a car. Sustrans produce maps of the whole network, available as books or individual maps: www.sustrans.org.uk.

The NCN's car-free sections are perfect for a family day out with the kids, the grandparents, or with a boy or girl friend, stopping at a pub on route for a drink and a meal. See www.bikeforall.net.

The National Byway is a 4,500-mile (7,240 km) signposted leisure cycle route round Britain. The Byway meanders round Britain, providing signposted direction along some of the most attractive and peaceful rural lanes, which carry traffic at only 2% of the national average level. In addition to the main route, there are 50 circular Loop rides. www.thenationalbyway.org.

There are many leisure cycling events organised across the country, like the London to Brighton ride and the Great Nottinghamshire Bike Ride, many of which are organised during BikeWeek in June. See www.bikeforall.net or www.bikeweek.org.uk.

Many of the events are also run for the benefit of charities such as Leukemia Research, so if you do take part, you could look into raising sponsorship money for a good cause.

Mountain biking

When the first mountain bikers hurled themselves down the mountains in California on converted cruiser bikes, few would have believed they were launching an Olympic Sport. Twenty-five years on, mountain biking has grown into one of the most popular sports in the world.

These days, mountain biking has become specialised into different disciplines; 'cross-country' is climbing and descending at speed on a steep dirt path, 'free-ride' is just having fun off-road taking on the biggest drops you dare, while downhill mountain bikes are great big, heavy, full-suspension monsters designed to go down very steep and rocky hillsides as fast as possible.

Mountain biking is a sport that does not depend on competition; it is a great way to enjoy the countryside while flying along a dirt track with a group of friends. It keeps you fit but also requires skill and is a test of nerve, as you learn to take on increasingly difficult descents. There are many trails that are perfect for mountain biking all over the UK, and the mountain bike centres recently built in Wales and Scotland are amongst the best locations in the world. www.mbwales.com, http://cycling.visitscotland.com/mountain_biking/mb_centre.

To get started, there are many mountain bike clubs, often run from a local bicycle shop. For information on the kit you need, local clubs or finding companions, see www.singletrackworld.com or www.bikemagic.com.

Road biking

The world's most famous bicycle race, The Tour de France, now has some sections in the UK. This is the pinnacle of road biking as a sport, but there are many road biking clubs all over the UK that cater for all levels of skill and speed.

A large group will ride together in a pack called the peloton. Riding closely behind another rider reduces the air resistance, so swapping places at the front of the group allows all the riders to go faster for longer. A weekend ride in an amateur club will often be characterised by the less fit riders dropping out of the group until only a few remain, the object being to stay with the pack as long as you can. Clubs are often based from local bicycle shops. For more information and forum pages see: www.britishcycling.org.uk/web/site/BC/bchome/home.asp www.bikeforall.net www.bikemagic.com.

Bicycle holidays

Taking a bicycle with you on holiday is one of the best ways to enjoy a new place. It provides excellent mobility in a city, so you can easily find a hotel, and it gives you the option to ride between towns, which means you get to experience the countryside rather than just whizz past it on a train. It is also a great way to discover remote beaches, villages or forests often missed by people travelling in faster modes of transport.

If you prefer to travel in a group, then there are many travel companies that offer organised bike tours to destinations all over the world. There is something for everyone, including many specialised tours for mountain and road bikers. The advantage of going on an organised tour is that you don't need to carry your

own luggage and equipment, which is ferried to the next hotel for you, and if you get tired or break down, a van following the group will pick you up or the group leader will help fix your bike. A professional tour company will also ensure the route is along beautiful, safe routes and is graded for different fitness levels.

If you are happy to carry your own luggage in panniers, and have a competent mechanic in the group, then it is just as easy to organise your own adventure. A week-long trip in a small group without a fixed itinerary, riding between villages, staying in guest-houses and hotels, jumping on the train or bus for some less interesting sections, can be a very pleasant holiday. Try to ensure that there at least two riders of similar fitness in each group; always waiting for one rider is not fun for anyone, while if there are at least two stronger and two weaker riders it is much less of a problem.

If you are very adventurous, then you can try a cycle adventure like coast to coast, Land's End to John O'Groats, across the Pyrenees, Alps, Andes or even the Himalayas. If you carry a tent and camping stove you can pretty much go anywhere. For more information on bicycle tours see www.inorbitt.com and www.bikeforall.net.

Extreme cycle sport

Bicycle Moto Cross (BMX) came to the UK in the 1970s and is still very popular with teenagers now, as well as with those who were teenagers in the 1970s and 80s. These strong, small-wheeled machines are used to make jumps either on dirt or in skate parks. It is extremely exciting, and equally difficult and dangerous. If you are already in your thirties or more then it is not recommended that you start to learn now. 12 and 13 year olds seem to have a lot more nerve than most 30 or 40 year olds.

Trials biking is a form of bicycle aerobatics, balancing generally on one wheel, either front or back, and jumping up onto rocks, fences, and down off roofs. It takes a lot of practice to gain the techniques to balance and make the jumps, although as the main skill is balance, it could be started in middle age if you had several hours a day to practise over a period of years. The basic Trials Biking technique is the Track Stand, which involves balancing on two wheels when stopped without putting your feet down. You can practise this while waiting at traffic lights.

Triathlon and Iron Man competitions include long sections of cycling, as well as running and swimming. You will need to be at the peak of physical fitness to compete in one of these, as it is usually harder than running a marathon.

Cycling to the shops

At weekends, going into town by bike will save you the bus fare or the parking charges, and if you have panniers you can carry quite a lot home if you go shopping; if the shopping doesn't fit onto a bike, then most shops will also deliver. A bicycle is ideal for popping down to the local shops to pick up a paper, some bread or milk or a bottle of wine.

Help give kids their freedom

Children can't drive. With more and more cars on the streets, our suburbs have become dangerous places for kids to play. Surveys show that most children want to cycle to school – paradoxically, one of the most congested times of the day is when the school run is being done.

You can help to change this. Most schools in the UK now have a Travel Plan. Committed teachers and parents are organising 'cycle-trains', where children cycle together to school and back under the supervision of an adult.

Organisations like Sustrans are campaigning for Safe Routes to School, and councils are listening, building cycle lanes and putting in 20mph zones, and restricting parking near schools.

Cycling with your children, or encouraging them to cycle to school and get the training they need to keep them safe, will keep them fit and give them freedom and independence to get about without an adult.

Cycling with children

Make sure your child has a high-visibility jacket or vest and wears a helmet that fits (it should be firm on the head without discomfort), and that there are cycle lights on the bike. Give the bike a maintenance check, make sure that the brakes work, and that there are no strange noises when your child cycles.

If you have young children, you can carry them on a child seat fixed to the back of your bike or on a cross-bar child seat. You can also get child trailers, which you strap the child into and tow behind your bike. Plan a safe route that follows quiet roads – if possible, try it out with your child at a quiet time of day.

Chapter 9

FURTHER INFORMATION

If you are looking for cycling companions, maps, training, group rides and events, or help with getting your bike fixed, there are many places where you can get support and advice:

Association for Commuter Transport offers advice, training and help to organisations considering a Travel Plan to encourage their staff to come to work by a sustainable means of transport. www.act-uk.com.

BikeBUDi – from Liftshare Liftshare is a software company that runs a car share programme for large employers. It has recently developed a similar software called BikeBUDi, where anyone can search for a cycle companion for their regular commute. www.bikebudi.com.

Bikeforall.net is a website with links, stories and information for people new to cycling, gathering together the most useful bike stuff on the internet. Bikeforall's editorial team bring you a collection of links and news, updated daily. You can rate the links and score them out of ten to give other users an idea of their usefulness. www.bikeforall.net.

Bike Magic A website with forums and tips for all kinds of cycling. www.bikemagic.com.

Bike Week A nationally coordinated week of events to promote cycling nationwide. www.bikeweek.org.uk.

Car-Free Day (22nd September) Once a year, as part of a Europe-wide initiative, people everywhere are asked to leave their cars at home and travel more sustainably. The day is often characterised by a series of events organised to promote sustainable travel. One of the most popular events is the car-free festival, where a road is closed to traffic for a day to allow the local community to enjoy activities like slow bicycle races, fancy dress, track stand competitions, and sometimes bands and entertainment.

Often the local transport authority will provide free public transport for one day, car clubs will give free membership, and there will be free bicycle checks and secure cycle parking. www.mobilityweek-europe.org.

Critical Mass started in San Francisco as a monthly ride for cyclists to get together and ride en masse around the city, so that for once cyclists would be the majority of traffic. The concept went global, and now there are regular masses in most major cities worldwide. The popular slogan associated with the movement is: "We're not blocking traffic, we are traffic."

The London Critical Mass is the biggest mass in the UK, although there are masses in Glasgow, Nottingham and many other cities. You can find links and meeting places for many of them on the Urban75 website: www.urban75.com/Action/critical.html.

The London mass is the best established, and meets on the South Bank outside the National Film Theatre between 6 and 7pm on the last Friday of each month. There can be up to several thousand riders. The police ride with the group and help stop the traffic to let the procession ride safely.

There are no leaders and no set route, but in amongst the twenty somethings there are usually a few bikes with sound systems on the back, some riders in fancy dress, commuters on the way home, and families. It is a great way to meet other cyclists and experience cycling around central London without worrying about the traffic. www.criticalmasslondon.org.uk.

CTC is the UK and Ireland's largest national cycling club, founded in 1878 as the Bicycle Touring Club, subsequently becoming the Cyclists' Touring Club. Its mission is 'to make cycling enjoyable, safe and welcoming for all'. CTC's work includes high-profile campaigning on behalf of all cyclists, made possible by the help and support of its 70,000 members. Membership of CTC provides advice, magazines and third party insurance. www.ctc.org.uk.

Cycle Aid helps cyclists who have been involved in an accident pursue their claims. Their advice includes cyclists' rights and responsibilities, the duties of the highways authorities, insurance, police, potholes, and how expenses for a claim can be paid. www.cycle-aid.co.uk.

Cycle Campaign Network (CCN) The CCN is a federation of about 65 cycle campaign groups with 19,000 individual members throughout the UK. The CCN runs a free registration scheme for Bicycle User Groups, and organizes twice-yearly cycle planning conferences in conjunction with the CTC. www.cyclenetwork.org.uk.

Cycling England is the national body which co-ordinates the development of cycling across England. Its aim is to create the conditions that will result in more people cycling, more safely, more often. www.cyclingengland.co.uk.

Cycling Scotland aims to bring cycling into the mainstream. It promotes public participation in cycling events, gives training to ensure people can cycle with confidence, and provides engineering services to ensure that cyclists are catered for on Scotland's roads and paths. www.cyclingscotland.org.

Cycle to Work Scheme This is a government tax incentive which allows employees to get a bike and accessories with up to 50% discount. The scheme works as a 'salary sacrifice', so the employee pays for the bike directly from gross pay.

It is possible for employers to set up their own Cycle to Work schemes, but due to the lengthy paperwork and difficulties navigating the tax system, most will use a third-party company to handle it. Such companies often have an agreement with bike manufactures and shops, who pay for their services, saving the employer the set-up cost. www.cyclesolutions.co.uk, www.cyclescheme.co.uk, www.cyclingengland.co.uk www.dft.gov.uk.

Cycle training There are now many cycle training companies that work with local authorities or employers to provide adult training at a subsidised rate. www.cycletraining.co.uk, www.companyofcyclists.com, www.cyclingfuture.co.uk. For details of training available in your area see www.ctc.org.uk.

Life Cycle UK A cycling charity promoting awareness of cycling issues. Projects include: cycle training for adults, teenagers and children; Health on Wheels – working with the NHS to provide cycling on prescription; Bike Ability – a project to promote cycling locally in the Easton and Southmead areas of Bristol; and Take a Stand – cycle stands for small businesses, community groups, schools, churches and voluntary organisations. www.lifecycleuk.org.uk.

Local authorities are responsible for developing cycle lanes and a cycle promotion strategy. The better local authorities employ a Cycling Officer to manage the various projects. They are often the best source of information on cycling, and will usually be able to provide cycling maps and details of local cycle groups and events. The Local Authority Cycling Association (LACA) is an association of cycling officers, and can provide information on how to find out what's available for cyclists at your council.

London Cycling Campaign is an organisation that promotes cycling in Greater London by raising awareness of cycling issues, campaigning to improve conditions for cyclists, and providing services for members. Services include: free automatic third party insurance, free legal advice, bike shop discounts, optional theft insurance, a bimonthly magazine *London Cyclist*, organised rides, and advice on all aspects of cycling. Although London-based, it has affiliations around the UK. www.lcc.org.uk.

The National Byway is a 4,500-mile (7,240 km) signposted leisure cycle route round Britain. www.thenationalbyway.org.

National Cycle Network see **Sustrans** below.

She Cycles A website with forums and tips for women cyclists. www.shecycles.com.

Sustrans is the UK's leading sustainable transport charity. Sustrans' vision is a world in which people choose to travel in ways that benefit their health and the environment, and it is the charity behind the National Cycle Network, Safe Routes to Schools, Travelsmart and other projects enabling people to walk, cycle and use public transport more. To find cycle routes where you live visit www.sustrans.org.uk or ring the information line on 0845 113 00 65.

TravelWise offers advice, training and help to organisations considering a Travel Plan to encourage their staff to come to work by a sustainable means of transport. www.travelwise.org.uk.

Urban Cyclist UK This web forum is a place to ask advice and offer opinions on everyday cycling issues. http://lists.topica.com/lists/urbancyclist-uk/read.

Index

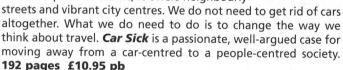